Michael Anderson's

Little Black Book
of
Songwriting

A Practical Guide for Songwriters

Cadillac Pink Publishing

Los Angeles

Michael Anderson's
Little Black Book of Songwriting

A Practical Guide for Songwriters

Published by:
Cadillac Pink Music
Los Angeles

Library of Congress Control Number: 2006904005

ISBN - 0-9786025-0-1

michaelanderson.com

Contents

About the Author
Acknowledgements
Forward
Introduction

About The Author

Michael Anderson

michael@michaelanderson.com

Michael Anderson is a songwriter / artist / producer / and author who has written songs for John Fogerty, Juice Newton, Pam Tillis, Phil Seymour, Rebecca St. James, and many others in rock, pop, country, and CCM.

He has been a staff writer for EMI and BMG Publishing in Nashville, as well as MCA / Universal and Criterion Music in Los Angeles.

Best known for writing "Maybe It Was Memphis" - #1 country single – recently placing #58 on the all time country love song playlist for CMT.

As a solo artist he has released six albums, two on A&M Records, two on EMI / Forefront, and two independent releases.

He has written many #1 CCM singles, and won a Dove Award for "Hard Rock Song of the Year" from the Gospel Music Association.

He is also an author – having written screenplays and books, including *"Shiloh: A Confederate Love Story"*, *"The Devil: A Postmodern Look at Nathan Bedford Forrest"*, and the film noir influenced *"Tin Angel"*.

He is a music business career and song consultant with the independent A&R company Taxi (taxi.com) and instructor at The Musician's Institute in Hollywood.

Acknowledgements

Thanks to Carl Byron for editing

Special thanks to:

Michael Laskow
Michael Lederer
Michael Lloyd
Eddie DeGarmo
Richard Green
Michael Puryear
Terry Manning
Patrick Clifford
Bo Goldsen
Michael Goldsen
Dan Howell
Delda Sciurba

Phil Seymour, Jeff Rollings, Victor Belmonte for the fire

And Jerry Burns – where ever you are - for the three-chord foundation

1. Foreword

Most people I meet in my business have a dream. They want to write a hit song.

Sometimes they've pursued that dream with no compromise, 100 percent, with a full time career in the music business. Sometimes they've pursued it on the side, a little bit at a time, over many late hours, weekends, and years while they held other jobs or even had another career.

But they hear songs on the radio and wonder, why is that a hit? Why couldn't my song be a hit?

Well, maybe it could. It's a long shot. But it happens. Somebody wrote every song you hear on the radio. And I'll guarantee you, each and every one of them wrote a lot of bad songs before they wrote that hit.

But each one of them had two other things going for them--the drive to keep making mistakes and learning, and eventually, an understanding of the elements of a well-crafted song.

A hit song can be a matter of luck; but before you even get to roll the dice on that, you need to be able to write a good song.

I have been in the music business a long time, taking it one step at a time, from absolute beginner, through struggling amateur, to having a measure of success with hit songs. Because of my practical experience people ask me for advice.

The following email is an interesting example.

Hi Michael,

Dean and I were thinking that as long as we were going to be in

Nashville in April, we could check into having 2-3 of my best songs recorded down there. It would have a truer country sound than my originals. Maybe with a better demo I might have a chance of getting published?

Isn't this the next logical step? I don't know. I work on my writing craft, to improve it, and as you know based on my demos, I'm not the greatest arranger on the keyboard, and my vocals are O.K., but not country sounding. I know what my strengths are as well as my weaknesses. That's what's going through my mind. I'm walking blind through this process. You've been down this road before. I haven't. I really need your advice.

I really do appreciate your mentoring me. You have given me hope that maybe I am getting better as a writer. Lisa.

Lisa:

I understand your frustration in trying to "crack the code" for success in this business. I have also sensed your willingness to set aside your personal feelings toward your songs and really listen to constructive criticism in order to get better. That is why I take the time with you to help when I can.

My opinion is, it all depends on the song itself. A clear vocal and guitar (or vocal and piano) demo of a great song is still a great song.

A full production of a song with structural flaws is still just a song with structural flaws. That's a lesson I have learned over and over again in this business. It's like building a house on an unstable foundation. You can build a mansion or cottage on that unstable foundation and it will never be right no matter what it looks like. I have seen many people waste ridiculous amounts of money making great demos of songs that had problems the production couldn't hide.

If you want to hear what your songs sound like with a full production, then the process you are considering in Nashville should give you that experience. It will be a learning experience, and that is usually a good thing.

But personally, I would make sure the songs are as structurally sound as possible before you take that major step.

Perhaps this book will help.

Introduction

I learned a long time ago to always consider the source of any information being presented. I look at who wrote something, and why, in order to assess credibility and perspective.

For that reason, I am providing this introduction as a general reference to give you some background, foundation, and perspective on my approach in this book. If you want to get right to the heart of the matter, skip this section and go to the next chapter. If you want to know where this book is coming from first, you can read on from here.

Who I Is

I am a songwriter and have been once since I was a little boy writing cowboys songs like Roy Rogers' before I was aware there was a "music business", publishers, or even money to be made from the endeavor. I wrote because, in the words of John Lee Hooker, "it was in me and it had to come out".

In classic American blues parlance there were two types of performers, the musician and the songster. Musicians played songs on an instrument with skill; songsters wrote songs. Songsters might also play an instrument, but their main skill was writing songs and words--meaning music with lyrics. It was the craft of writing lyrics that set songsters apart from musicians.

I am a lyric guy. I have studied lyrics, listened to lyrics, written lyrics, and loved lyrics all of my life. Many of the people I admire in this business are "musicians." They think in terms of music and playing an instrument. I have also been a "musician," playing an instrument in bands.

But at heart I am a "songster," I write songs. And I appreciate a well-written song with a great lyric very much. The advice in this book comes from that perspective.

I remember soon after my first major label album was released I was doing a radio interview, and the DJ asked me how I write songs.

It's a question I have heard repeatedly over the years. My short answer is, I don't know how not to write songs.

I started with those little cowboy songs, then, at an early age began writing poetry (always with the idea of turning them into songs). I began writing lyrics as a teenager for local bands that needed someone to write the words for their music.

I learned to play bass guitar and played in local bar bands in my 20s, and began writing songs myself about that time. I went through the stereotypical trials and tribulations of a rock musician trying to make it in this business. After moving to Los Angeles, I eventually achieved a measure of professional success by signing my first staff writing publishing deal.

I have made my own records, collaborated with other people on theirs, and worked with other songwriters professionally for over 25 years. I have several number one songs and awards, and a body of work that I am proud of. I have sizable song catalogs at five major publishing companies, released four albums as a major label artist, and also have put out two independent releases.

I also studied screenwriting and have written screenplays. I love the form and scope of film. I will refer to very interesting parallels between screenwriting and songwriting from time to time in this book.

Hollywood

When I moved to Hollywood in the late '70s I learned that one of the best ways for people to break into the movie business was to be a "reader" - the person at a studio or agency who was paid to read the scripts that come in and do "coverage" for the boss who didn't have time to read everything. Essentially, that meant writing a critique.

Some of the best screenwriters, directors, and producers learned their craft in the trenches reading good and bad scripts, and discovering for themselves what worked and didn't work.

In that spirit I have worked for many years as a consultant and screener for Taxi, an independent A&R (artist and repertoire) company based in Los Angeles.

At Taxi, I provide coverage for other industry professionals on songs and artists that I screen. I have listened to song after song for hours, days, weeks, months, and years. During the past few years, I would conservatively estimate that I have critiqued more than thirty thousand songs.

I have also recently been added to the staff at the Musician's Institute in Hollywood as an Artist Development instructor doing one on one songwriter consulting.

Over the years I have formed some definite opinions about songs and songwriting. As a result, people ask me for advice and request consultations about their songs and careers. This book is intended to set out the foundation of my perspective on songwriting.

Obviously, everything in this book is my opinion. I don't have a corner on the market for truth. Many other songwriting resources, books, programs, and seminars exist. Take them for what they are worth. Someone else's perspective may well differ from mine. I'm going off what I have learned in my experience.

Perspective:

Songwriting As Art

Songwriting is an art form, not a formula. Good songwriting is a delicate balance between talent and skill. I'm defining talent as a natural ability and as the essential ingredient in creating artistically satisfying results. But when it comes to translating talent into success in the music business, the key is determination. Stubbornness.

If you have no talent for songwriting, nothing in this book will change that. If you have no determination, forget the music business. I have seen people with very little talent go a long way in this business (listen to the radio), and I've known very talented people who couldn't survive the ride.

People are talented or gifted in different ways. Some have the knack for drawing or painting; I can't draw a straight line with a ruler. Some people are great dancers; I've never been comfortable on the dance floor. Some people are good at becoming another character and acting, or directing groups in a theater or film location setting. Everybody seems to have something.

If you have some natural ability for songwriting, I hope this book will help you focus and maximize your gift, give you another perspective, and help you craft better songs on a more intuitive level.

Like all living art, songwriting is a form of action that is impossible to codify and force to conform to strict rules and conventions. Every time someone attempts to lay a law down in stone for an art form, the next great artist comes along and flagrantly and successfully violates that rule. That's why it is art, not science.

For every basic elemental guideline of songwriting presented in this book, many exceptions surely apply. I'm simply offering observations and suggestions, opinions and perspectives defined through the lens of personal experience. Take or leave anything you like.

Songwriting, like any art form, is also an individual path. Reading about it, going to seminars, listening to others speak about it can all be encouraging, enlightening and even inspiring. But ultimately it is you actually doing the work yourself--participating in the process--that teaches you the most about the art form.

Songwriting As Play

One aspect of songwriting that I cannot over emphasize is that it should be fun. I love writing songs. Sometimes I can forget that due to business pressures, financial responsibilities, criticism, and because my own ego can get in my way. But the memory of the joy I felt writing a cowboy song as little kid comes back to me and I realize that songwriting is how I feel right with the world. I'm mentioning that to you because I need to hear it.

Like any craft, you learn a little at a time. Sometimes learning is a painfully slow process. If you are a beginner you probably won't write the greatest song ever written immediately after reading this book. But that next song may be the best one you've ever written. It is a step-by-step process. The journey of a thousand miles begins with the first step and all that...

Find your joy in the process. I have written some very gratifying songs. I enjoyed the feeling of accomplishment and satisfaction when they were finished. But it was the process, the excitement of doing it that I always enjoyed the most. When you enjoy what you are doing it shows in the finished work.

Appreciate your gift. Concentrate on where you are and the next step, and your final destination will be getting closer. You may never get there. You may get there and not like it, you may get there and it will be everything you dreamed of. Or you may be there now.

Spiritual Aspects of Songwriting

In order to understand the perspective of this book you should know that I believe that art is spiritual, that it is an expression of that part of our nature that seeks to rise above the mundane, the physical, to reach for something more--the understanding of life, love and purpose. I strongly believe that all human beings have within them talents and gifts to express their own unique perspective on life.

An analogy I have heard is we are like different prisms taking in the source of life, one white light, and putting out different colors and patterns. I like that.

The music business exists to remind us that temptation, corruption, evil, hell, and a devil (usually the head of A&R) also abound. I'm kidding of course. Sort of.

I believe we are social, as well as spiritual creatures. Our nature is to seek answers to the big questions of life, death, and love, as well as to live, work, interact, and help each other through this difficult journey of life holding each other up, encouraging each other, contributing to the betterment of our community and the common quality of life.

Besides, if it weren't for other people, who would buy your CD?

Everybody has a natural, healthy desire for self-expression, an entirely individual way of communicating a personal vision of the world. C.S. Lewis said we read in order to know we are not alone. I believe we create in order to communicate on that level. Not only to call attention to our condition and ourselves, but also to be truly happy we are inspired to enrich and encourage others in their journey.

And to buy their CDs.

Creating art is one way of fulfilling that spiritual need. Art is communication involving an expression by the artist and appreciation by the audience of an otherwise inexpressible feeling. Great art expresses that feeling in a way that nothing else can. Through art, we see and hear things from another perspective.

Life is hard. We need each other, and art is one way that we realize, through nonlinear communication, we are not alone. Someone else has been through it, others out there have made it, and we can too. There is a purpose and reason for it all. And it can be fun.

Why did I write this book?

For the past few years, I have been advising, consulting and expressing my ideas on songwriting in increasingly focused ways to a greater number of people. I have felt for a while the need to write down what I have learned for anyone interested in the essence of songwriting more than the detail.

I have heard theories and ideas of song craftsmanship from other writers, some of which I have found useful and informative, others of which have seemed overly technical rather than helpful to songwriters simply trying to understand the essentials of their craft and how to better their abilities. My intent has been to focus on the framework and elements of a song.

I have never been an intricate detail guy, which may be one of my faults. I like to learn about the foundations of something, the basics, and then work my way through it on my own, finding my own way. I am one of those guys who won't stop and ask directions at first if I am lost. I'd rather learn how to find my way (learn the process of becoming unlost) than actually get to where I am going.

That approach to songwriting has had interesting effects over the years. I have been told I have a unique, very recognizable style that hasn't changed fundamentally over a career spanning 30 years. I suppose that is good and bad, or possibly neither. It is my way though.

I am not necessarily an art for art's sake guy. I'm sure there is something noble in being the artist who does it for personal satisfaction only. But I like to blend my art with commerce. I like being paid for a song. For that reason, this book has a practical side to it that will also focus on being able to communicate effectively with an audience.

The Importance of Form/Structure

I am not a fan of formulaic music, or any kind of art, which uses paint-by-numbers processes in order to achieve a predetermined reaction. However, I make a vital distinction between a formula and a structure.

I believe that there are fundamental song forms, and I will discuss some that I consider to be foundational and which I believe represent the essentials of song structure. But I encourage your experience with form to be liberating in possibility, and not limiting in imitation.

I have found the basic pop song form to be similar in discipline to haiku poetry, three chord blues, or the sonnet.

These are all seemingly rigid forms that have endless variation and possibilities within the structure. A structure of possibilities rather than limits.

The beauty of a great song is bringing all of the elements, consciously or unconsciously, to fruition through the process of writing and crafting; to deliver an emotionally satisfying experience to the listener the way a great film, book, short story, painting, or performance does. Unlike those art forms, a pop song does it in about three minutes. That takes focus, structure, and a plan.

Form is a very involved topic, and many good books and courses go into far greater of detail on its intricacies than I do here. This little book is intended as a very basic guideline on the elements of songwriting, and is meant to give the purposeful songwriter a solid foundation for fine-tuning a song.

Conclusion:

I will not attempt to teach you how to write a song. You either already do that or you don't. It is your gift or it is not. If it is, this book should give you guidelines that will help you write songs in ways that more effectively communicate your inspired ideas.

My purpose here is to lay down a basic foundation and perhaps a philosophy about the art of songwriting so that when you express "what is in you that has to come out," the results are clear and compelling.

This is not a "get rich quick writing songs for fun and profit" book. It is a "how to recognize essential song elements and use them more effectively to craft your ideas in a way that other people will understand them within the structure of a song" book. That was too long for a title though.

Many other books speak in depth about the business and craftsmanship side of this equation. My recommendation on that score is John Braheny's "The Craft and Business of Songwriting". For delving into the artistic and spiritual side, Julia Cameron's "The Artist's Way: A Spiritual Path to Higher Creativity" is one of my particular favorites. But for the basics, read on.

Chapter 1

Title

ti-tle n.
A name or descriptive heading that identifies a composition.
A word or phrase or sentence that is used to designate a work and thus distinguish it from other works and often indicate the nature of it's content.

Title awareness

Most non-professional songwriters do not understand the importance of the song's title. In my case, it was a gradual process to finally appreciate just how necessary an effective title is.

First Titles

When I first started writing songs, like most beginners, I did it pretty much by instinct--learning by doing. I honed my craft by trial and error. And, at first, my audience was myself--the easiest critic in the world.

The first real test of a song though was playing it for other people. Nothing reveals the strengths and weaknesses of a song like the immediate feedback of an audience. You embarrass yourself into writing better songs the next time.

Whether you're in front of an audience of one or of many, the entire feel of a song changes when you play it for someone else. It's uncanny how you hear it filtered through others.

When you play a song in an amateur or semi-professional situation by itself there is no compelling need to identify the song in a unique way by the title. If it is the only song you're performing, or even as one of a few, it is usually easily identified.

Live Performing

When you get to the stage of performing songs live as a collection of some kind, there is more of a need to identify the songs individually. First off, the band or accompanist needs to know what song you're doing. Then, unless each song is introduced with its title and/or a story, the audience may instead identity a song by a distinguishing characteristic, such as a repeating hook line, a guitar figure, the one with the flute solo, the one where you forgot the words, or the one where the Mormon Tabernacle Choir drops from the ceiling in a balloon. That would be a hook, but it may not be the title.

You want people to remember the song. They want to identify it, and it is to your benefit that they can refer to your song by the title. But even at that stage it isn't quite critical.

"What's the Title"?

Then you progress to the stage where you are submitting songs in a demo form to industry professionals for either evaluation or consideration. In most cases what you are submitting will be categorized with many other submissions from other writers and will be competing for the attention of the A&R type who would be listening to the material.

I remember when I first started dealing with industry types; I was always a little surprised and even somewhat irritated when they would ask, "What's the title?"

At that time I didn't understand what that could possibly have to do with the quality or viability of the song. I was used to audience reaction to the song. I didn't quite understand that circumstances had changed. An audience had already heard the song in most cases when it wanted to identify that particular song.

In the case of industry professionals, time is valuable. They are still deciding whether or not the song is worth listening to in the first place. And they get a lot of information about the song from the title.

When I started writing for Nashville publishers the title became an even bigger focus. I sensed somehow that the title was some kind of code that told them how good the song was going to be. Many years later, through my own experience in A&R, I found they were right.

Title Code

Back when I started I would often write songs from an idea that didn't have a title. It would be a "Chuck Berry-ish" thing, or a "Stones-y" thing, or a country ballad, etc. That is how the song would be designated in my mind. A title would organically flow from the idea of the song at some point.

In one way I was correct. A good song idea is usually a good title. But what an industry professional knows is that a good title usually means a good song idea.

When I first started listening to other people's songs for evaluation, I usually needed to get through the intro (see the Intro section in Chapter 8) to catch the vibe of a song, but after a while I could pretty much nail it from the title. It finally dawned on me as I listened to other people's songs what my publishers were seeing and hearing in the title years before.

The title says much more than most casual listeners realize. An experienced song professional can discern a song's depth by the title the way a psychic can tell fortunes by reading tea leaves.

A song is an idea, and a title describes the idea. A well thought out, clever idea can usually be hinted at in the title to pique the interest of the listener and give some indication or preview of what is to come.

There are certain things an effective title does:

Qualities of a Good Title

Identifies

The first thing a title does is identify your song. It names your song in the way a name identifies a person. For instance, if everyone were named simply "José" with no other names, it would be difficult to identify a particular "José" from any other "José".

Many songs have very similar titles. They become hard to identify and keep track of on a business level. (Imagine the categorizing headache of a common title to BMI, ASCAP, or Sony Publishing). But more importantly, to the listener, common titles are not memorable or unique.

Song titles like "I Love You", or "I Miss You", or "Don't Leave Me" or other generic, nondescriptive titles don't give your song a unique identity. Even more important, to an industry professional, a lackluster title will also indicate a lack of imagination that will more than likely be a characteristic of other elements of the song--no need to waste much time on that one.

The title is the first impression that industry professionals have of your song--and you almost always only get to make one first impression—unless they perhaps hear your song first, such as in a live situation. Still, even in that case, these industry pros should still be able to discern your title well enough to remember what song it was they heard. On occasion, artists have wanted to cover a song of mine that they hear me perform. They identified the song by the title.

The title names your song. It distinguishes your song from all the other songs the listener hears. And, if it is sitting on an industry professional's desk waiting to be listened to, ideally the title should imply something interesting about the character, attitude, or feel of the song that makes that person want to hear it.

Designate and Distinguish

One of the most overlooked aspects of a title is the ability to convey in one small phrase an element of the song that gives it a distinguishing characteristic.

Does the title say something about the song that is unique or special to that song? For instance, "Yesterday" conveys a sense of longing in one word. "I Love You" shows a lack of imagination and will probably be developed in an obvious way. "I Miss You" also seems very obvious, but with a slight twist, "I'm Not Missing You At All" (in which the lyric actually shows the singer is missing her very much) tells the same basic story in a fresh, interesting and memorable way.

I have always liked the title "I Want To Hold Your Hand". That title was different and interesting in a teenager way for the time. Many listeners of the Beatles in 1964 were in the stage of actually wanting to hold hands.

But if you listen to the story line, the singer actually wants to hold her hand while telling her "something." It's a bit of a tease. That "something" is the obvious, but it's not stated until the bridge. This is a classic example of a title doing many things at once. The main thing it does is to identify the song and get the listener's attention in a clever, immediate way.

Many titles however do not do that. Picture yourself as an industry professional with a desk piled with demos bearing titles such as "I Love You", "You Broke My Heart", "Please Come Back To Me", and "Take Your Tongue Out Of My Mouth (I Was Kissing You Goodbye)." By the way, that last one is an actual song title.

Which would you listen to first? Which piqued your curiosity and jumped out of the pack?

There are a lot of songs out there. Sometimes the title may be your song's selling point. It should say as much as possible, on every level, about your song. It is the Zen of your song. But mainly, is it interesting?

Indicate the Nature of Content

Here's the bottom line: how much can someone take away from your title in terms of feel, style, approach, attitude, relevance, and interest? Does your title make someone want to hear the song?

A good song can have an OK title. But usually a great song has a title that says something special about it; it gives a feel of the song, and gets the listener ready for what is coming.

Outside of some esoteric, creative title concepts, the following section offers some very basic ideas to consider when evaluating your song's title.

In my experience there are several areas where songwriters could be more effective with titles.

Problems with Titles

Missing Titles

One missed opportunity I see frequently is using a title that doesn't appear anywhere in the song. For instance, what would you think about a love song with the title "To Julia" that doesn't feature the name "Julia" anywhere in the song itself? Julia might know whether or not the song is about her, but the rest of us would have a hard time understanding that.

Or consider a song written about a cold winter day, titled "In December", but nowhere in the song is December specifically mentioned. Perhaps we're supposed to assume that the day described in the lyric is occurring in December, but January and February are also winter months with many of the same cold weather characteristics.

The writer assumes in both cases that if the listener knows the title and hears the song, then the two will be connected. However, by not having the title in the song the opportunity for clear connection is lost.

Lost Titles

Sometimes a writer will bury the title in a part of the song where it is not apparent. I have heard songs with the title only used in the opening line, or in the body of the verse, or perhaps once at the end of a verse.

More often, the problem is that the title will be in the chorus somewhere but not in an obvious focal point. It might only feature in a passing line where it can easily be overlooked. It is usually most effective to have the title in the opening line or last line of the chorus, or preferably both.

Boring Titles

Another basic thing some writers do is just repeat the same line over and over again throughout the chorus in an effort to "drive home" the song's hook and/or title. That can get redundant very quickly.

Even a basic chorus idea can usually use some theme and variation to break it up. That variation can be as simple as a different third line in a four-line chorus, where the first, second, and last line of the chorus are the same.

Questions to ask yourself about the title of your song:

Could someone listen to your song and tell what the title is?

If not, what would they call it when calling the radio station to request it or look it up to buy it?

Is your title interesting enough that someone would want to hear the song after first seeing or hearing the title?

<u>Notes:</u>

Chapter 2

The Groove

Groove
1. *a strong beat or rhythm in music (slang)*
2. *to play jazz or dance music with a strong beat (slang)*

Feel
1. *to touch somebody or a part of somebody's body for the purpose of sexual gratification*
2. *to experience or cause an emotion or physical sensation*
3. *to be instinctively aware of something, usually an emotion, that is not visible or apparent*
4. *to be deeply affected emotionally by something*
5. *an impression of something gained through touching or being touched by it*

Beat
1. *to hit somebody or something with repeated heavy blows*
2. *to make natural short rhythmical movements (refers to the heart or pulse)*
3. *to hit a drum repeatedly to produce a musical rhythm or a signal*
4. *to establish a musical rhythm, for example, by clapping hands*
5. *a rhythmical sound or movement made by something throbbing or pulsating (often used in combination)*
6. *an act of striking one thing against another, or the sound of one thing striking against another, especially repeatedly and rhythmically*

7. a single element of measured time in a musical piece or poem. Beats occur at regular intervals and are the rhythmic and metrical foundations of music.

8. the dominant rhythm in a piece of music, especially a strong rhythm in rock music

9. beat or Beat typical of or produced by members of the Beat Generation

It's hard to image now, but a lot of the uproar over rock and roll music in the fifties was the beat: that infectious R&B influenced groove that inspired an entire group of poets, writers, artists and performers to be called the Beat Generation, and led a teenaged John Lennon to call his new band the Beatles.

White parents thought the primal beat of rock and roll would put their impressionable, hormonally excited teenagers into a catatonic, euphoric, trance-like state, and influence them to experiment with drugs, become sexually aroused, reject the cultural values of their society, and become more like Negroes.

They were right.

The Heartbeat of Your Song

The groove has been the heartbeat of music since the first pre-historic man (I'd bet it was a man) started pounding out rhythms on hollow logs for people to dance to for religious ceremony or fun (these are very similar pursuits outside of puritanical societies). It is no coincidence that for years the basic criterion that the teen audience on American Bandstand used when judging a song was if it had a good beat and they could dance to it.

Victor Belmonte, the first great drummer I ever played with, taught me that 4/4 time was the natural groove of a heartbeat. He said the groove of a song communicated directly to a human heart. That can be a powerful element of a song.

African Influence

Africa is the motherland for what has become the central fundamental heartbeat of American music. Many cultures around the world depend on a groove for much of the distinctiveness of their music, and many of those grooves have found their way here. But because of the history of this country, African rhythms have become the primary foundation of American music.

It is no coincidence that much of American popular music's foundational spiritual home has been the South, where slaves were brought from Africa and had to survive under inhuman conditions. The beat--the spirit--was a source of strength, identity, and communication. It has become an American characteristic.

Religious ceremony was one of the few activities allowed the slaves in the early days, and many of the primary elements of their cultures were incorporated into the trappings and language of their white master's religion in order to be expressed. Through that spirit the music and the people survived. The foundational root of American music--black gospel music and its secular offspring, the blues--can be traced back to the days of slavery.

Blues music was the product of its environment. Its homeland is the brutal Mississippi Delta, home of most of the greats of the genre such as Charlie Patton, Tommy Johnson, Son House, Willie Brown, Robert Johnson, and McKinley Morganfield who migrated to Chicago and became Muddy Waters.

Soon after 1900, New Orleans became the birthplace of jazz with its rich mixture of influences. According to Wynton Marsalis, in Ken Burns' excellent documentary "Jazz," the *roux*--or the base--for the gumbo that became New Orleans jazz, was the blues from the Delta floating down the Mississippi River to the port city.

From the Delta and New Orleans, the migrating blacks of the South brought the music through Memphis to the big cities of the North--to Chicago, Detroit, and New York.

Influential record labels--Stax and Sun in Memphis, Chess in Chicago, Motown in Detroit, and major labels such as Columbia in New York--spread the gospel of American black music: early blues, jazz, rhythm and blues (R&B), and fifties rock and roll (exemplified by Little Richard and Chuck Berry).

It took the British invasion of the sixties, and British musicians who worshipped American black music, including the Beatles, the Rolling Stones and Led Zeppelin, to awaken the American public's consciousness to the vitality of its homegrown culture.

American pop music today, from dance to rock, hip-hop, heavy metal and even country music, is heavily influenced and in some cases simply derivative of the foundational African feel.

The African connection in rock, hip-hop and R&B may be obvious. But consider also the case of the Mississippi-born and raised Jimmy Rodgers, "The Singing Brakeman," the acknowledged founder of modern country music and the very first inductee to the Country Music Hall Of Fame in Nashville. He was a white man who, when heard today on his 1920s and early '30s recordings, sounds to me more like a bluesman in the mold of his contemporaries such as Blind Lemon Jefferson or Robert Johnson. He seems to have far less in common with major country figures of subsequent eras like Hank Williams, Garth Brooks or Tim McGraw.

Groove and Spirit

It is also no coincidence that religious rituals, ranging from those of Southern Baptists to various pagan sects, begin with music or chanting or singing of some kind. The beat or drone opens the spirit, bypasses the reasoning faculties and turns off the turmoil in the consciousness. The individual soul unites with the collective consciousness and forms a spiritual connection in the ritual.

Church services, rock concerts, wedding bands that get guests dancing, and even local bars with a band in the corner have that same ritualistic aspect in common. Music is an integral part of the ritual of the spirit that unites people, and the groove is the element that connects the body and the spirit. It is soul music.

Genre Feel

Every style of American pop music has its own particular accent or stylistic groove--an identity stamped into the feel--that sets it apart.

If you are born into a class or social group with a particular style of music and have been a part of it all your life, a certain type of groove or feel will seem natural to you. It's usually something you don't have to think about.

But if you're planning on pitching your song to a particular musical genre, and you're not already a member of a community--whether ethnic, racial, religious, or regional—that is closely identified with that type of music, it's a good idea to immerse yourself in the elemental grooves and feels, the beats of the style of that genre. You have to connect on that primal, nearly unconscious level to be authentic to the audience that has that type of music already in its blood.

Your Groove

Listening to a song without a groove is like listening to a speech by somebody without an opinion--what's the point?

Listen to your groove. Listen to the beat. Do you move your head or feet, sway or jump to the movement in your song? Does it engage your heart? A focused groove can show up problems in meter, timing, phrasing and structure.

One easy way to make sure your groove is at least average is by using any of the currently available myriad of looping programs and/or CDs with digital samples of various rhythms along with a sequencer. Even an inexpensive drum machine can be helpful in creating a solid groove; although getting a human "feel" from that type of device might be a challenge. Another way to get a song started or focused is to play it to a strong groove you like from a song in the style or genre that you intend to pitch.

Remember, your groove allows the listener to get into your music and bypass the intellectual critical faculties. It should move into the heart and spirit elements of the music.

A groove or feel that is obviously wrong for a genre is apparent to a music business professional and to the audience for that music.

I have found the most common missed opportunity in a song in terms of groove is a soft, unfocused, generalized feel with no discernible identity. The wrong groove identity in an otherwise good song can be changed, but a lack of identity can rarely be fixed.

Is Your Mojo Working?

The best test I've found of whether or not your groove or feel is working is watching as other people listen to your song.

Did they smile as the beat started?
Are they moving?
Are they swaying to the beat?
Are they into the song before the first lyric is delivered?

If not, you have lost a prime opportunity to connect with your listener on a primal, unconscious level and set the listener up for hearing your song with one defense down.

Notes:

Chapter 3

Melody

mel·o·dy n
1. *a succession of single notes of a different pitch arranged in a way that it is a recognizable entity – the principle part of a piece of harmonized music*
2. *a series of musical notes that form a distinct unit, is recognizable as a phrase, and usually has a distinctive rhythm*
3. *the linear structure of a piece of music in which single notes follow one another*
4. *the primary and most recognizable part in a harmonic piece of music*

Definition

The melody of a song is what people used to call the tune; a recognizable series of individual musical notes of different pitches with a distinctive rhythm delivered in a way that makes it unique as a phrase.

A melody is the series of notes that you recognize when playing the notes of a song on one hand on a piano or keyboard, as single notes on a guitar, or that familiar, distinctive phrase of a song you hum.

It is also the musical phrase your lyric uses as its foundation for delivering your song. A sense of melody is one of the most difficult aspects of song writing to teach. It seems more than any other element, a sense of melody is the most innate and natural.

Melody is a simple concept. In Western music, the octave (the span of all the white and black keys between C and C on a piano keyboard, for example) includes twelve individual notes, or pitches. The foundation of conventional

Western harmony and melody, as formalized during the 18th century--principally through Johann Sebastian Bach's works—is a system of major and minor scales derived from specific sequences of those pitches.

For example, the C major scale consists of all the white keys, between C and C on a piano keyboard. That's the basis for "Do Re Mi", the famous song from "The Sound of Music." All key signatures in Western music, from C major through the entire cycle of major and minor scales, consist of seven pitches.

The five "left-over" notes that aren't included in each scale can often be used to add something distinctive to melodic lines and harmonies. For instance, if your song is in C major and your melody line is cruising along using only the white keys of that scale, notice what happens if you throw in a B-flat (the black key below the C) at some point. The melody acquires a different character.

Without getting further into musical theory than necessary, the main point is that from Beethoven to rappers, composers and songwriters have been using the same system of scales for centuries. From Cole Porter to Neil Young, Robert Johnson to Charlie Parker, Billie Holiday to Yoko Ono (well, maybe not Yoko, there's always an exception).

Yet it seems that beginning songwriters often overlook melody as an essential aspect of contemporary pop songwriting.

A strong melody is one of the most distinctive elements of a memorable, successful, and long lasting pop song. Think of Frank Sinatra and Tony Bennett's hits, the Beatles' songbook, Disney movie ballads and Christmas carols. They all have recognizable and singable melodies.

Singers and Melody

A good singable melody shows off a singer's talent in a way no other element of a song can. Singers like melodies that give them a chance to showcase their special gift--their voice. For this reason, it's a usually a good idea to craft your songs' melodic lines in a way that will appeal to singers to whom you might be attempting to pitch your material.

All singers like to exhibit their range and tonal qualities, but I have found female singers especially like a melody with a strong top end, a lot of emotional peak in chorus melody, or a big ending to stretch out and dynamically deliver the song.

If your song has the elements that take advantage of the singer's strengths, and really shows off his or her abilities, your song might have a better shot at getting recorded over one that may have a stronger lyric, better structure, a connection in the publishing company, or even a co-write with the artist. Artists need hits and they want to look good doing them.

Singing Melodies Live

Having the ability to perform isn't a prerequisite for being able to write good songs. A lot of very famous songwriters were not necessarily good performers. But many of them were.

I have found the ability to get in front of an audience and embarrass yourself into writing better songs is an invaluable tool in learning the craft. I recommend it. Even if you're only performing on songwriter nights or at a local café.

You learn a lot about songwriting in general, and melody in particular, by singing on stage. There is a range in the human voice that carries and delivers emotionally in front of people. If your melody is below that, it stays under a singer's ability to get the feel across, and if your melody is unsingable the emotion will be lost. Singing your songs live to an audience will teach you what those vocal feels are so that you can incorporate them in your melodies.

It is important to remember in this age of multitrack recording studios, Pro Tools, microphones, loud electronic music and P.A. systems, that the natural elements of vocalizing have been developed over thousands of years, and people like good singing. It resonates in our hearts and in our spirits.

It is also an important lesson to understand the natural range of the voice and use it to advantage in the melody of your songs.

You can also learn those ranges from recordings. By careful study you can learn what keys and melodic ranges different singers work in to the advantage of their ability, tone and delivery style.

Testing Melodies

One of the easiest tricks I teach people for focusing a melody is to play it out in single notes on a piano (a real acoustic piano being best for some reason). If you can articulate a melody that is recognizable and perhaps even pleasant and memorable you are way ahead in making your song distinctive.

Another good test of your melody is to play your song to someone else and see if they can hum your melody back to you. You may be surprised how difficult it is to write a natural, flowing melody that someone remembers and can sing back to you. (If they can hum it back to you a week later you may have a hit).

That's why one of the most effective ways of writing a song is just singing out loud to yourself, for instance in the car. That method has a lot of things going for it. You can sing out uninhibited (assuming you are alone – ignore the stares from other drivers – you may be rehearsing for an opera for all they know); you are doing something else (hopefully concentrating on the road) so sometimes it flows more naturally than when you are concentrating or forcing it, and you can feel a natural flow and get a sense of the obvious sing-along quality of your melody and song.

I sometimes take a small cassette recorder in the car with me for working out melodies and harmonies on songs I am still in the process of writing or recording. You'd be surprised at how much time you spend in a car (especially in Los Angeles) and how concentrated your time working on a melody or harmony can be.

Sectional Melodic Considerations

The shape and feel of melodic lines are also affected by where they appear in a song. Sometimes it is effective for the melody to be a bit straighter in the verse and more flowing in the chorus, sometime the opposite. But ideally there should be sectional contrast and perceptible melodic differentiation between the verse, chorus and bridge; and the melody ideally should lift to its emotional and melodic peak in the chorus (preferably on the hook/title phrase of your song).

During the ending, the melody can then also change up a bit in intensity and emotion, with some theme and variation as well as vamping opening up the song up for a big finale. Again, feel and experience work there.

Common Melodic Problems:

Sing-Songy Melodies

Melodies by developing songwriters can tend to sound too simplistic, limited in variation, and overly repetitive in a sing-song sort of way. That kind of approach can work for children's songs. Children enjoy easy melodies like that. But a lack of sophistication will limit your pitching opportunities.

Unfocused Melodies

One of the most difficult kinds of melodies to listen to is the unfocused melody that doesn't seem to end naturally as it twists, turns and meanders but doesn't seem to have a tonal center, goal or focus. The phrase is hitting notes, but they feel unrelated and don't take the listener anywhere interesting. An unfocused melody is confusing and frustrating.

Listening to a song with an unfocused melody is like being a passenger in a taxi lost in a strange city with twisting, turning one-way streets, signs in a language you can't read, bad traffic, in the heat when you are hungry.

Good Melody

A good melody has a flow. It delivers smoothly and effortlessly. Nothing gets in the way to hinder it. You can hum it easily.

A good melody is emotional; a good melody feels familiar. It is like catching a perfect wave for a surfer, and it flows as it takes you where it goes in a satisfying, pleasant way. It runs smoothly and effortlessly. It feels natural, like there is no other way, no other order of flow in the notes or expression that could say that particular thing better at that moment.

A good melodic sense in a song is a big indication to an industry professional hearing your song that you know what you are doing on a craft and artistic level.

Questions about your melody:

Can you hum your melody?
Is it interesting? Does it flow?
Can someone hum it back to you?
Is there some sectional contrast?
Is there a melodic "hook"?
How singable is it for a singer?
Does it show off vocal range and tone?

Chapter 4

Lyric

Lyric n.
1. Intense, personal poetry– lyrical – passionate, enthusiastic
2. the words of a song, especially a popular song (often used in the plural)
3. a short poem expressing personal feelings or thoughts

Definition

Lyrics are the words to your song. They can seem similar to a short poem but they serve a definite function within the pop song form. Lyrics tell the song's story. But within that simple definition are conventions as well as countless variations on telling your story effectively.

The word "lyric" originally comes from the Greek idea of personal poetry accompanied by the lyre, a stringed instrument. From the Greeks, to David in the Bible composing songs (Psalms) with lyrics on a stringed instrument, the romantic troubadours of the middle ages, the lone cowboy on the range with his guitar, the itinerant Mississippi bluesman jumping trains in the 30's, through Woody Guthrie and Bob Dylan, to MTV unplugged, the singer/songwriter with an acoustic guitar derives from a long tradition. And technically, even though it is "plucked" with hammers activated by a keyboard, a piano is a stringed instrument.

These archetypes are the ancestors to our contemporary idea of singer/songwriters and their acoustic guitar or piano writing songs. That image is very much alive today, especially in Nashville. All art forms have a language and a structure that is used for the communication of ideas within that form.

Whether it is painting, film, poetry, dance, cooking, or music, the language of an art form is a means of both self-expression and communication. For the intended audience, there are expectations that provide the basis for the communication between the artist and audience.

The contemporary pop song structure is tight, focused and consists of sections. Those sections are verse, chorus, bridge, perhaps an intro and usually an ending.

Once the form (structure and language) is understood and accepted by artists and audience alike, the audience can relax a bit and judge and/or appreciate the artists' expression and the artists can focus on telling their story.

Basic Writing Suggestions

Books and Screenplays

I have learned a lot about song structure in writing screenplays and books. All three expressions work within the conventions of their respective forms. For any songwriter, I recommend reading a book on the structure of screenwriting. You'll find a world of information and good advice for getting to the point in dialogue, which is essentially what a song lyric is.

Writing in long form for stories or books is also good practice for the songwriter. It feels good to be able to stretch out and not be limited by a timed form like a screenplay or song. And it can also help you appreciate the economy of the song form, the focus of expression, the nuance--similar in focus to haiku poetry, the three chord blues, or a Shakespearean sonnet.

Notepads

Some people recommend keeping a note pad with you at all times for writing down ideas. I won't discourage you from doing that. But I should let you know that I've read through some of those notepads and I've found very little of any interest in them.

I have found that if I get a really good idea, one of two things happens. The idea is good enough to remember until I get to where I can write it down, or I decide it is so good it is worth the effort to find something I can use to write it down with right then and there.

When I lived in Nashville you could go anywhere in town any afternoon and find songwriters sitting at tables alone, over coffee, seriously writing in their notebooks.

I remember meeting Harlan Howard one afternoon at the Sunset Grill in Nashville. He and I were alone in the bar. We talked about songs. He had a drink in his hand. He knew the history of country music; he wrote most of it. (He'd had a hit song every year since 1958 and he also coined the phrase "three chords and the truth" in describing country music). He knew more about the sales and chart positions of my hit "Maybe It Was Memphis" than I did.

I had read an interview once where he discussed all the lyric ideas he got from waitresses and women in bars, and how he had scraps of paper--restaurant and bar napkins, backs of envelopes, and so on--with ideas on them. With all his hits I found myself thinking he could have had an official notepad if he thought it important. He didn't have a notepad in his hand. He had a drink. It wasn't coffee either.

As I write this I have recently finished putting together two records for a friend of mine, the late Bryan MacLean. Bryan was a songwriter and the guitar player from the 60's band Love.

I met him much later and we became friends. I lived with him for a while. In all the time I heard him working on songs, playing and preaching, I never saw him write anything down.

In putting together records from literally a trunk of cassette tapes, his mother and I never found a lyric sheet or music written down. Hundreds of amazing songs, nothing written down. I remember him playing for hours and never looking at a note.

And yet his music is intricate, the lyrics detailed and structured. They were all from his head. Inspired.

There is nothing wrong with keeping notes and files, and organizing your ideas and songs. But I don't think notepads are necessarily a key to the process.

On the other hand, when I am working on lyrics, I like to use one of those extra long yellow legal pads – give myself a lot of room to write down a lot of stuff and edit it down later.

Theoretically a computer word processor should work the same way. But it has been said that in theory, theory and practice are the same thing, however, in practice, they are not. Songwriting is like that.

Simplicity

Here's one more observation before the main points: in this day and age, when we are overloaded with information that is rarely relevant, simplicity is becoming not only desirable, but a necessity for effective communication.

People with nothing to say often talk too much. Songwriters are the same. A good idea is a rare, precious element in a song. It is what the song should be all about.

Good development of a good idea has a logical, linear, clear, emotionally and intellectually satisfying flow; as if there is no other way that very thing could be said any better.

The art is saying just what needs to be said, no more, no less.

Song Lyric Structure Overview

Verse

The verses of your song are where you tell the story and set up your chorus. There are many ways to do that. A couple of basic ways are the story form, the obvious chronological order, or finding another internal sequence that is artistically and emotionally satisfying.

All the elements of linearity, focus, clarity, and a foundational idea should be in place and considered when you get to structuring your verses. The verses should set up your chorus; they should relate directly to it in a poetic way. The verses should also build chronologically, emotionally, or in some other way so there is an actual reason why the first verse is first, the second is second, and so on. Ideally, there should be an internal structure that tells the story and supports the chorus.

If you have a chorus that says something, the verses can tell the how, where, why, what, etc., of the chorus. The verse can set the mood and tell the story.

If a verse later in the song veers off a bit too much story-wise, or if you sense you are trying to bring in other elements that are not quite in the flow of the other verses but which tell an important aspect of the story, consider making those bits into a bridge. It should have a different melody, feel, and chord structure to contrast with the other parts of the song.

If you change a verse up too much it tends to break the flow of the song and confuse the listener. It is better to break it completely with a bridge and give the difference a purpose.

Chorus

The chorus is your song's emotional high point. It is the part people should sing along to, and remember. The chorus is the articulation of the point; it is what the song is about.

A song structure has dynamics that have an internal flow and sensibility; they flow to and from the chorus. As a general rule I have found structurally that having the chorus hit at about the one minute mark of a song feels about right.

Starting the song with the chorus can be effective also. As they say in Nashville, "don't bore us, get to the chorus". If you want to hook your audience with the idea, the chorus is the place to do it.

There are many forms for structuring a chorus, but one effective structure is starting and ending the chorus with the title/hook of your song. You want to get the idea cross, but you don't want to beat the listener up with meaningless repetition. Another form is ending with the title/hook in the last line. This device doesn't give you the repetition but it does offer the chance to build to your lyrical (and hopefully emotional) climax.

Starting your chorus with the hook and not repeating it in the chorus rarely feels balanced in my experience. By the time the final statement of the last line is made, the impact of the first line seems dissipated. Something about having the last word leaves a stronger impression.

Title

There is a whole section of this book on the title, but here in the lyric chapter I'll mention that the title ideally should be an integral part of the your chorus. It should be the focus, the idea, the distillation of the song in a phrase. The title should be the bedrock, the bones your chorus is structured on. It should be the centerpiece. It could also be the first and last line of the chorus.

I know, I know, the Beatles' "A Day In The Life" breaks that rule. Lots of songs break lots of rules. When you are titling the greatest song of your career, on arguably the greatest pop album ever made, you can bend the rules a bit too.

See, I'm flexible. (But I'd also point to every Beatles hit single as an example of the obvious title rule).

Hook

The "hook" can be many things in a song. It can be a catch phrase in the lyric (usually the title), a musical phrase, a melodic phrase, or even something like the "Whooo" in the Beatles "I Want To Hold Your Hand", or "Yea Yea Yea" in "She Loves You", the dance in "The Macarena", or Jimmy Page's guitar solo in any number of Led Zeppelin songs.

A memorable song has something that sticks with the listener and distinguishes it from every other song. That identity is a key to your song becoming unforgettable.

Bridge

The bridge lyric serves a slightly different function than the verse or chorus. Ideally a bridge lyric should take a look at the theme and idea of a song and give it a different POV or provide perhaps the "moral" of the story from the perspective of an outsider looking in.

I always liked the stories about Lennon and McCartney writing the bridge for each other's songs, thus providing a different feel within a consistent stylistic context.

A few questions you can ask yourself about your lyric.

Does your song have a good idea?

Can you tell the idea to someone else like a film idea pitch? Are they interested in it? Or is it another version of the same thing that has been written over and over?

What about the subject matter? Is the song about something a lot of people would care about? There is nothing wrong with writing for yourself alone or a specialty market, but be aware you are doing that and don't get frustrated or disappointed when no one cares about your song.

Love songs are prevalent because in the prime music buying time of life that is the biggest emotional crisis facing the audience. Falling in love, falling out of love, getting hurt--all of these emotional experiences are interesting to people who buy records.

Is what you are saying interesting and relevant to your target audience? Tastes can vary considerably from person to person. Life is full of variety. But there are general areas where you can be relatively sure someone may or may not be interested in the topic of your song, and which target audience may or may not find it interesting. For example, a country audience isn't usually interested in a song that's set in Minnesota. You might want to change the locale to Tennessee, or Texas, or a similar place.

Say you've written a song about Uncle Fred, for instance. Uncle Fred may be important to you, his family and friends, but no one else really cares. That song may be wonderful to the people who know Uncle Fred, but unless the song transcends Uncle Fred and hits a note of universal relatability to a broader audience (which can be done), very few people will find song's subject matter compelling.

Other subjects may or may not be interesting to different degrees. A really incredible song about a subject people are not interested in might not be as popular as a less well-crafted song about love. What you are writing about, and what you are saying about it, can be as important as the craftsmanship.

It's sort of like the real estate mantra: location, location, location. What is your song's idea? Does anybody care about that idea? Is it important, and does it say something relatable to your listeners?

Can you state the theme?

Not necessarily what it says – but what it means. Does it have a fresh twist, a new observation; say the same thing in a new or different way? A song can have a subject and theme. They are not necessarily one and the same. For instance, the subject of the Beatles' "Eleanor Rigby" is a woman named Eleanor Rigby, but the theme of that song is loneliness. The subject of Robert Johnson's "Terraplane Blues" is his car, but the theme is sex.

Your audience may not be aware of all this, but if you are, it helps focus your lyric.

I have heard many people say they just write lyrics that feel like something to them but different people can have their own interpretation of what the lyric means. I suppose that's OK , but it does nothing for me.

I have found for most contemporary pop song pitching that a clear, accessible, linear lyric that has depth, emotional feel and a compelling story is a stronger pitch.

Does your song have a story?

Does your story actually say something? To paraphrase an old screenwriter adage, "the king was walking with a pretty girl" is an observation, but "the king was walking with a pretty girl as the queen came around the corner" is a story.

As good as it is to have a strong idea, the idea needs to be set up and delivered for maximum effect; that is the art of story telling. You can tell a narrative factually for instance--just giving a sequence of events--or you can build it like a ghost story around the fire at a campout when the woods echo with mysterious sounds, the moon is full and everyone is edgy anyway. That is what makes the difference between a reporter and a storyteller.

People enjoy the emotional ride, the process of the story unfolding, the building of tension and emotion. In almost any movie, you know the good guy is going to win and the bad guy is going down. The interesting, entertaining part for the audience is how it happens and how the ride feels. A song is the same thing. Give your listener a ride.

Does your lyric story have a beginning, middle, and an end? In other words, does it develop in a linear (or any other) way? If your song is saying basically the same thing in each verse, from beginning to end, why should the listener be interested after the first verse and chorus?

Structural patterns--internal forms that lend a coherency to the whole--are very important in lyric development. For instance, if your song is about colors, each verse could deal with a different hue: blue, red, and yellow.

The last verse is usually where everything comes together somehow--where there can be a " twist" (a rainbow, for instance in the case of the color song)--a turn of phrase or word that carries a meaning other than what was obvious and that deepens the emotional feel.

You can also disappoint the listener with what authors call the "ghost in the machine" effect. An example of that would be tying up the story line with an artificial device or event to play on the emotions without a good set up, such as the listener finding out that the loving wife and mother with two kids in the first couple of verses and chorus is dead in the bridge. The listener feels tricked without a normal dramatic arc, some kind of hint or foreshadowing of what is coming.

Can the listener understand it?

A lyric shouldn't be simplistic, but simple is good. A song serves no artistic purpose if it is not understood. My classic reference is the Zen of Hank Williams, Sr. You know and understand every word of a Hank Williams record. And so did every country listener. And yet there is an emotional depth and truth in nearly every line. That is genius.

Does your song say what it means clearly, in a simple, easy to understand way? Could you read it to others and have them know not only what you are talking about, but also what you are trying to say about it?

You might have someone read the lyric out loud to you and explain what it means to him or her; how do they perceive the idea?

Having people outside of your writing process read your lyric can provide valuable insight. They are usually more dispassionate and less emotionally attached to the material and can see it more for what it is than what you want it to be.

Problems With Lyrics

Is the lyric narrative focused?

Does your lyric stay with the story line and develop the idea gradually line by line, and section by section, to a coherent, whole?

One thing I learned in screenwriting is the idea of each line of dialog being its own world, and how the nuance, the phrasing, all the possible meanings convey the idea. Each line of dialog should flow towards the next and the next, keeping a coherent, connected thought building and moving along in an interesting way.

One method of focusing a lyric is to start with the title/idea /hook and work backwards as well as forwards through your song and see if every line and idea points directly toward the development and exposition of your theme. Can your listener follow the development of the idea clearly? You may know everything about what you mean but the listeners only know what you tell them.

Sometimes a lyric is like a conversation when someone talks and talks and you kind of know what they mean but you don't really understand exactly what they are saying. Or they speak with a strong accent and you can't quite get what they are saying. It gets frustrating. A listener won't stick with that type of expression.

A song lyric is emotional and connects with both the head and the heart. You don't want anything that breaks that flow and connection.

Imagery Focus

There should be a logic and pattern to your imagery. Imagery is an expression that uses a mental picture or concept. Make sure your metaphors and images work together to build the theme of the song and connect with any imagery and metaphors used within the chorus itself.

Imagery and details that don't serve to keep the story moving forward only confuse or throw the listener off track in trying to understand your story line. Overly flowery lyric writing with a lot of poetic imagery can get confusing to the listener. Try to keep every word, every idea, every verse, flowing forward and supporting the main idea of your title/hook/chorus.

Be ruthless in editing. A great line may sound good on its own, but does it help tell the story of your theme and make a point? Imagery is a powerful tool in a lyric. Don't let it confuse or lose the listener.

Does your lyric have a linear flow?

As has been apparent, I like telling a story from beginning to end, and I think the listener appreciates that form. But sometimes just putting your most interesting verse first can keep the listener's attention.

As a matter of style, more conversational lyrics have a more contemporary feel and authentic vibe about them. Conversational lyrics are lyrics that have the nuance and rhythm, the feel and personal connection of having a conversation with someone--a more informal communication in contemporary vernacular.

Older, more formal styles of lyric writing can be more flowery and poetic sounding (although conversational lyrics can have a poetry of their own). Non-conversational lyrics can also tend toward more theoretical and philosophical tones that lack directness; they can feel sort of over your head. Sometimes the idea is more or less apparent, but the way it is expressed feels indirect and vague. Ask yourself: are your verses linear in telling the story, do the verses build in a logical way in themselves, moving forward the idea?

Can your listener follow along, line by line, with the developing idea, to an interesting resolution and satisfying artistic statement that speaks to the heart? People like artistic pieces of a puzzle being skillfully put together to create a whole picture.

So many songs I hear meander. They go in one direction, change gears, turn a corner, and then come around the block to say something. It's more difficult for the writer to intentionally say something clearer, but much easier for the listener to understand.

Does each verse build toward and add relevant information to the theme? (Not just saying the same thing in a different way as the verse before and after it, but also adding something to the story). It doesn't have to be a novel; in fact it shouldn't be a novel. But it should strive toward haiku (or the Zen of "White Christmas").

Orphaned lines

Even when the basic idea is there, another tendency I see are "orphan" lines; individual lines or phrases that stick out. They're unconnected in any way directly to the lines around them in following or developing the story idea. These lines often manifest as clichés or metaphors that mean kind of what the flow is going for but they do it in an awkward or clumsy way. "Orphan" lines come off feeling like a lack of imagination, laziness or reaching when the right idea isn't easy.

Perspective

This may seem basic but I run into it: does your speaking perspective, the POV (point of view) of the lyric, stay the same? In other words, if you speak to a "you" in your lyric, is it the same "you" in the last verse as in the first? People sometimes change the perspective, for instance by speaking to a "you" that is the girl (or guy) in the song, and then addressing the listener as a "you" later in the song. It tends to confuse the perspective for the listener.

Clichés

Linear flow can also be broken by clichés: overly used, too-familiar expressions or ideas. They seem to stop the flow in a very subtle way; your song stops building, moving forward, and expanding. The cliché turns off the listener's attention. If you aren't making any effort to deliver a fresh, new idea why should someone else put any effort into listening?

Sometimes a cliché will work (that is how it originally became a cliché), especially if it is used in a new way, or twisted to make it different somehow. But the main thing is the idea. If you have a good idea, everything can work together to put it across. If the song is lacking a good main idea, then stringing together clichés and generic phrases feels empty and boring to the listener.

Metaphoric Continuity

Be careful also of metaphoric continuity. A metaphor is a figure of speech in which a name or quality is attributed to something else that isn't literally the same.

For instance, she can have snow white skin and fiery eyes. You can roll down the highway and probably even fly down the tracks, but if you head out on the highway to keep that train a rollin' till your ship comes in you might be mixing more metaphors than the listener can keep up with logically. You might want to go through your lyrics and pick one aspect of your metaphoric imagery and stay with it through your song.

Laundry list

Another flow breaker is the laundry list lyric in which each verse and line is just a list element to fill space and doesn't move the story forward but treads water beating the idea to death (speaking of mixed metaphors).

For instance, a typical list song could be one about loving someone everywhere, with each verse filled with the names of states. A laundry list form can be effective, though, if there is an internal reasoning to the order of the list or a build of the emotional or relevant content.

Paul Simon's "50 Ways To Leave Your Lover" is a clever send up of the form where he actually makes the laundry list itself compelling with distinctive phrasing and interesting rhyming scheme and delivery.

For the most part though, songs that employ the laundry list form become very repetitious and predictable very quickly.

Poetic magic

Then there is poetic magic, the touch that transcends what is being said and takes the listener to what is being meant. It conveys an emotional vibe. Those moments usually come in flashes of brilliance or conversely, when you just write and write and then go back and edit and filter down to the essence of what you are trying to say. That's when the whole becomes more than the sum of the parts.

<u>Notes:</u>

Chapter 5

Music

mu·sic n
1. sounds, usually produced by instruments or voices,
that are arranged or played in order to create a pleasing or
stimulating effect

I am not going to get into a lot of music theory here.
Musicians spend endless hours and entire lifetimes
studying music theory. But music theory isn't songwriting.

In pop songs there are three kinds of musical structures
you need to know: ballads are slow songs, up-tempo are
fast songs, and mid-tempo are somewhere between the
other two.

That's enough technical jargon for now.

Publishers love a great ballad but rarely want one because
there are so many, publishers are always looking for a good
up-tempo song unless you are pitching them one, and mid
tempo songs are like lukewarm water.

As far as a more specific analysis of why certain chord
structures, harmonic progressions and melodic shapes are
more likely to result in an effective song than others, a lot of
dry, technical books get deep into those topics.

I get very bored reading them. What I will recommend is
using your ear and your heart. If those don't work well for
you there isn't a lot anyone can teach you about music
anyway.

Play Live

My fundamental advice in terms of learning music theory and developing your own musical language for your songwriting is to learn to play an instrument (that includes voice), and to use it live, in front of people as a performer.

Learn songs, learn styles and learn to play the songs you like, even if they're from one of those easy chord type songbooks.

Then steal like a politician with a government contract.

Learn to play that instrument, perform live, get up in front of people and be lousy. Keep learning and get better. These are not only the most invaluable lessons for songwriting, but for life. The humiliation, embarrassment and rejection will also prepare you for dealing with the music business; especially for pitching your songs.

Audiences that talk loudly over your performance, ignore you or don't applaud (or fail to even materialize) are the milk of human kindness compared to what you will encounter in the music business.

There, you'll be considered lucky to even land a brief meeting with a highly-connected, corporate checkbook-toting industry professional who has appointments backed up and telephone lines ringing constantly. This person will barely look up from his desk to deliver a quick dismissive one liner about your song: "I'm not looking for a ballad/up-tempo/whatever your song is, right now."

You will be humbled in this business. You will be rejected. Diane Warren songs get passed over way more than they get cut. Beat the rush: start early dealing with rejection and get used to it. It's like dating. Everybody goes through it, there are no shortcuts.

(Ever wonder why some big stars act like jerks? I think it's because they were treated like dirt on the way up and once they make it to the top being a jerk is their revenge. But cut 'em some slack. They will probably be on the bottom again soon enough.)

When you stand on stage and perform, whether in a honky tonk, a church or a wedding reception, you get to know what people react to. You find where your strengths and weaknesses are, you feel how audiences react to different grooves and styles, you know when you hit their "monkey nerve" (see Chapter 10 for an explanation of that term). All of these lessons will show up in your songs.

One of the biggest lessons I had about music came when I played bass in bands, sometimes five sets a night, six nights a week in local bars.

There was one country band in particular I remember. We mainly played small dive bars with postage stamp stages, tiny dance floors and the smell of stale beer, cigarettes and adultery in the air.

I was young at the time, was really into rock and roll and played country mainly just to perform and make some money. I was so embarrassed I didn't even tell my "cool" rock and roll musician friends. But I couldn't have paid for better experience.

By playing Waylon and Willie, Elvis, Creedence, George Jones, and Hank, Sr. to drinking, dancing, cheatin' working class crowds who were loud and vocal about their likes and dislikes (especially after a beer or six), I learned quickly what moved them and what didn't. One night on stage in a place like that will teach you more about country music than a lifetime of listening to the radio.

You never forget that feeling. That experience stayed with me, even much later when I finally went to a Nashville and wrote country songs on purpose.

When trying to find your voice for telling your story in your songs, performing live and playing your songs for other people is where you will develop that sense of what's right and what isn't, what works and what doesn't. You will also gain confidence in what you are doing because experience is the best teacher.

Three Chord Blues

I will offer one lesson in the very foundational, basic music structure of the American pop song. As you've probably noticed by now, I am a foundational guy. I like getting to the bottom of something and understanding how it works.

The fundamental music form of American music is the three chord blues. (Here we go back to the Delta again). I am not going to explain it here because you can't learn it by reading about it. It is like sex or Zen; so basic it defies literal, accurate description in words--but once you do it, you get it.

To understand songwriting, from blues to country to soul to gospel and most anything contemporary, a songwriter should have at least a rudimentary understanding of the three-chord blues form. Most American pop music is a direct copy, descendant or some variation or derivation of this fundamental form.

Get a Chuck Berry record and have someone show you the chords if they're not obvious to you, or get 'em from a chord book. Learn the basics and put 'em to work over and over and over. Make the form yours, because you will find it at the root of nearly every American style and genre. It is the basic American music structure--what everything else is built on.

I was initiated into the knowledge and taught the basics by a grizzled old bar band guitar player when I was a teenager. He was probably 30 or so at the time, living with a waitress he had gotten pregnant—she was from the local club he was then playing--until he went home to his wife in some other town. Welcome to the blues, kid.

He started me on bass because it was easier than learning how to play chords. On bass I could play one note at a time. He showed me how American bar band blues and rock music was built on the three-chord form, and how almost any song could be conformed basically to the style.

There are endless variations on the form, but the simple three chord Chicago blues or especially Chuck Berry rock and roll can give you hours of practice time and open a world of practical music theory. The basic 12 bar blues will get you started not only in writing, but understanding the musical form of American music.

If you can't find a grizzled old guitar player to teach you, I would recommend finding a basic blues and/or rock and roll guitar or piano book and getting that form down. It is very simple, yet endless in possibilities of stylistic and structural variation. And the structure can be so simple that at an early stage you can work on feel.

The pregnant waitress is optional.

Stealing

I have found that a song's music can be basic, but it has to support the melody and be distinctive in rhythm, chord feel, and playability. Again, back to playing your songs live and being proficient (or at least sufficient) on an instrument. (Again, I include your voice here).

I sometimes advise people to practice songwriting by taking the chord structure and melody from a song they like and writing their own lyric to it to see how the pieces are put together. One advantage in that method is if something's not working you know it's you. If you are lucky you may come up with something new that sounds different.

Study the structure of your favorite songs. Figure out why you like them. Use the things you learn. There is a reason why certain conventions work, why certain chord progressions are repeated song after song, why certain tempos feel right in certain genres and get used repeatedly.

Steal those.

I once read an interview with Keith Richards in which he said the Rolling Stones were always just imitating Muddy Waters as best they could, but they weren't good enough at it so it came out sounding different, i.e. as themselves. If they had been really good musicians they might have ended up playing in Holiday Inn lounges. Ray Charles started out by imitating Nat "King" Cole. Elvis Presley wanted to be like Dean Martin. Paul McCartney does a great Little Richard. You might define a whole new genre by not being good enough to imitate your hero.

Musical Style

One main point I often stress to aspiring songwriters about the musical content of their songs is that it be stylistically defined and focused in the genre they are trying to pitch.

I hear musical approaches to songs that come from every direction. With all of the advances in sampling, processing, sequencing, and looping, and computer software programs that even write your music for you, the one key ingredient that can't seem to be bought is a compelling sense of stylistic definition and focus.

The seemingly endless variety and possibilities available these days via technology are not necessarily good things. For most beginning songwriters, a computer songwriting program is like giving a three-year old a thousand piece puzzle to put together (with tiny pieces).

There are all kinds of musical genres out there and each has developed over long periods of time. Each has its own language and attitudes. The music is one area where it can all come rather prepackaged with loops and samples. Writers very often seem to think they can mix and match pieces of styles like accessorizing a new car. But that usually comes out more like mixing ice cream and pepperoni. Maybe not even that good.

Be conscious and aware of what you are writing.

Pitching Genre

I have people play me their songs all the time and then ask, "What style/genre is this right to pitch to?" I want to answer, "If you don't know, how should I?"

That's like a guy inventing something and then asking the patent office what it is. It's the creator's job to define function. That's not to say the market won't redefine it later, but originally there should be some focus.

How often do you suppose the music industry invents a new stylistic classification and genre for songwriters who don't know what their songs' style might be?

If you answered "never," you're catching on.

In screenwriting, the standard advice is, "know your ending," and write backwards.

In songwriting, know what you want to say, know how you want to say it, then say it. Make it clear. If it is clear in your head, and you know what you are doing, it will be clear to your listener.

If it's not clear in your head, jam on some three-chord blues for a while. I've heard that's what Eric Clapton does. Hasn't hurt him.

<u>Notes:</u>

Chapter 6

Structure

struc·ture
noun:
1. a framework, or other object that has been put together from many different parts
2. a system or organization made up of interrelated parts functioning as an orderly whole
3. the way in which the different parts of something link or work together, or the fact of being linked together
verb:
1. to organize or arrange something so that it works as a cohesive whole

The structure of a song is the framework, or bones the song is built on. A good understanding of the fundamental elements of a song's structure and how they work together is essential in fitting the parts together to achieve the desired effect and to make sure your song is built on a solid foundation.

The following is my basic overview of the most vital points you'll need to know in order to structure your song well.

Length

One of the foundational elements of the structure of a song is duration: how long the song is and how each section fits within the framework.

These days, pop songs are generally around three and half minutes in length, although some are clocking in closer to the four-minute mark. Some beginning writers think those durations are artificially short; how can you say something complete in that amount of time? I point out that most of the early rock and roll pop radio classics by Elvis, the Beatles and other greats are only around two and half minutes long, yet emotionally they are mini-symphonies. It's about working within the structure.

There are reasons why pop songs are so brief. One reason for the time limitation is that the early acetates used for recording only ran for a few minutes.

Another reason was the advent of radio and the idea of programming with commercials. For those and probably many other practical and artistic reasons (including audience attention span) the pop song form has come down to us as a convention that actually does feel natural when done right.

The original record business was based on the single--a song with a duration between two and a half minutes to four minutes (on average) that was sold everywhere from filling stations to furniture stores. These songs were heard and promoted on a then contemporary invention--radio.

That song form has held up through technological changes from recording wax drums, through 78, 45, and 33 1/3 rpm vinyl disks, to cassette tapes, eight-tracks, CDs, mp3's and beyond. It has been a very resilient form.

Except for a brief flirtation with long form songs in the 60's during the hippie freeform FM radio days, the format has stayed essentially the same since the 1920's.

Today, with the consolidation of radio stations and centralized programming, airtime is more valuable that ever. So the compact pop song form is alive and well as a standard in the radio and record industry.

It will probably hold up through whatever technological advances in digital radio or packaging forms become available too. It has some momentum now.

Elements of Pop Song Structure

The structure of a pop song is usually made up of a mix of elements including the intro, the verse, the pre-chorus, the chorus, the bridge, and the outro.

Intro

The intro is where your song is set up. In the same way that title can be an important indicator of your song's potential viability for an industry professional (see Chapter 3), the intro can tell the story of your song before the first lyric starts. There is a feel, a vibe to an intro that transmits a particular energy.

The elements of a song, the groove, the feel, the musical texture, the atmosphere are all presented (or introduced) in the intro. There is a tight, deliberate, attention-grabbing confidence to a good intro that makes you want to hear what is coming next.

The intro is your first chance to get your potential listener's attention. Or lose it.

One way to lose listeners' attention is to bore them with an overly long intro. A pop song intro gets a bit long after about 17 seconds. There isn't a lot to do with an intro after that. Set your song up and get to it.

Another waste of time is an intro that has nothing to do with the rest of the song. You want to set up your listener for what is to come. Get 'em interested. Don't confuse 'em.

Verse

The verse is the body of your song. There are several elements to a good verse. The prime importance of the verse is telling the story in a clear, linear, logical fashion. Even if the actual language is impressionistic, the main point is the communication. A contemporary song might be loaded with imagery, or it can be direct and conversational. But the story line--what you are trying to say--should be communicated in a clear way.

Ideally, the story line and structure should also build and connect on the song's basic idea in a logical or sequential way so there is some kind of dramatic arc that keeps listeners hooked and takes them from one place to another.

Mere observation can be interesting, but if it doesn't tell a story that develops it will get boring. That's a big mistake to make in a three and a half-minute song.

In terms of structure the verse usually comes after the intro, although another effective structural technique is to start the song with the chorus. Most songs however roll straight from the intro into a verse.

The verse generally goes about 45 seconds when there is no pre-chorus. In songs with a pre-chorus, the verse is generally closer to 30 seconds long.

Pre Chorus

A pre-chorus is a building section that comes after the verse and before a chorus. It usually has a dynamic ramping-up quality that leads into the chorus and provides some sort of transition.

The pre-chorus can be a repeated section used for continuity throughout the song, and it can have a distinctive melodic or thematic pattern that signals the beginning of the chorus to the listener.

If a pre-chorus is used in a song, the song's structure will usually not need a bridge to provide another section of contrast and relief. The song will probably be long enough without the bridge if its form includes a pre-chorus.

Chorus

The chorus is your focus; it's the part of the song the listener should remember. The chorus is the point of the song, the emotional and musical climax, and it is where the whole song is delivered.

I have found the one-minute mark of the song to be about ideal for getting to the chorus. In a three-minute song that gives you three choruses.

The chorus ideally should have the hook/title prominently showcased. It may repeat the hook/title as a first and last line, or repeat it throughout the chorus (but that's a less contemporary device).

Dynamically the chorus should have a lift effect; a melodic, sonic and emotional feel that brings the section to another level and separates it, gives it contrast in comparison to the verse, pre-chorus or bridge. A chorus that soars is a beautiful thing. It takes your emotions as well as the lyric idea to an emotional peak.

Bridge

The bridge is a change up section, usually following after the second chorus. It's designed to provide some contrast and an opportunity to try something different within the context of the song's vibe.

Bridges commonly go to the relative minor of the root key of the song (in the key of "G" major for instance, the bridge might begin on an "Em" chord), and give the feel of a break in the action with a gradual build back into it. Lyrically, the bridge can come from a different POV (point of view) and tell another aspect of the story in a way the verse and chorus maybe can't without losing continuity and focus.

Instrumental Break (or Solo)

Most contemporary song forms will include an instrumental break or instrumental solo of some kind. This usually comes after the second chorus or bridge, although sometimes it can be effective to come out of an instrumental break into a bridge. The idea is to work within the dynamic build and flow of the song.

The instrumental break can use the basic form of the verse, which then leads nicely into a chorus. Alternately, the break could be over the chorus structure. In that case, a big outro could follow the instrumental section, or for an effective dynamic contrast, the song could quiet down at that point and the final verse could deliver a more intimate lyric idea.

I have found solo instrumentalists seem to prefer playing over the chorus structure because it gives them a chance to vamp on the emotional high point of the song. I have found it is a good idea to make your players happy whenever possible.

It can also be very effective for the instrumental break structure be a slight variation of a verse or chorus, or combination of the two. Emotionally, you want the instrumental section to "say" something musically that can't quite be expressed lyrically in the rest of the song.

Outro

The outro of a song, the section after the last chorus, or the repeat of the last chorus, is a "let it rip" section that can take a song to its conclusion with a flourish. Usually the chorus or a variation of it keeps repeating and fading to the end.

In many songs based on pop structure, the outro is little more than an after thought. But there is an art to taking your song out with a bang and leaving the listener wanting more, such as hearing your song again. In some styles, such as black gospel, the outro is practically the beginning of the song because all of the emotional build really starts to take off at that point.

I have found that by vamping an outro during the writing process, and really listening, you can sometimes come up with dynamic and emotionally focused material that can then be reincorporated into the body of the song. This process can be especially useful in developing a more effective delivery of your chorus title/hook melody, and it can also help you to better determine the optimal range of the melodic lines.

The outro can be a good place to loosen up and feel where the song wants to go on its own. Sometimes they do write themselves. That's when it starts getting really good.

<u>Notes:</u>

Chapter 7

Style

Style

noun:
1. The distinctive / distinguishing way something is done, presented, written, constructed – the distinctive character of a type of music.
2. The fashion or pattern – a mode or way of fashioning in a customary style.
Stylized
verb:
1. to use convention for a calculated esthetic effect in the rendering of a subject.
2. a distinctive and identifiable form in an artistic medium such as music, architecture, or literature
3. a way of doing something, especially a way regarded as expressing a particular attitude or typifying a particular period (often used in combination)
4. the way in which something is written or performed as distinct from the content of the writing or performance
5. the ways in which written material is presented

Verb transitive:
1. to give something a particular shape or design
2. to bring something into conformity with a particular style

I've written this section as a broad overview of the attitude of style in songwriting, not as a detailed exposition of genres, styles and techniques. The best way to understand particular musical classifications (pop, country, R&B, blues, gospel) is to listen to them a lot. Or be born into that culture. Describing music with words is like trying to describe a color to a blind man.

So for the purposes of discussion here, I am talking about generalized considerations of style in crafting your song.

Song Style and Fashion

Any discussion of style and fashion, classifications and classifying of songs usually generates resistance from *artistes* who feel insulted by the idea of their work being "labeled".

My response is simple: get over it. Everything is labeled in one way or another and that is the way of the world. The business runs that way.

Your art does not have to be influenced in any way by that labeling. You can maintain your artistic purity and keep your vision if you like; it is, after all an ostensibly free country. Many artists have lived and died protecting the integrity of their work. Van Gogh is a prime example.

Consider how many other great creative spirits died broke and in obscurity. If you choose to be one of them I admire you very much and appreciate your courage.

The rest of you can continue reading.

The style of a song is determined by many different elements. For the purpose of this section I will defer to the way the Billboard charts categorize contemporary pop styles. Each of these categories has its own target audience, and songs in those styles usually have a recognizably distinctive way of being presented, written, produced and marketed

Style, in terms of contemporary pop songs, is not fashion. Style can last a long time; fashion by definition is temporary. I recommend writing in a style, but I advise avoiding writing in a fashion, which is too ephemeral. By the time your song is out there, the fashion has changed.

The fashions of contemporary pop music change more quickly than any book can track. You might want to keep up with fashion through trade magazines, most of which also offer online editions.

In the following section, I am going to address style in a broader sense.

Categories

Certain categories of music have more or less remained constant in charting. There is a general pop category, an edgy teen pop one, a basic country one, an R&B one, and a more or less generalized gospel category broken down into black and white subcategories.

In the broadest sense, pop (i.e. "popular") music is the music people buy. For that reason the Top 100 chart lists many different styles and songs that also appear on charts that track specific categories. The reason charts are broken down into categories further than just the main overview pop chart is for marketing purposes. Niche markets or submarkets have been identified that can be targeted for radio, advertising, or other forms of exploitation.

When you write a song it can be classified at many different stages. You can write for a target market (focus), you can end up with a song that fits a certain market (rare), or someone else may label your song for you (not always the way you intended it).

In some cases, over time a song will gradually fit into another category as fashions change. But in order to be marketed—and this is an absolutely essential point to keep in mind--your song has to fit somewhere.

That idea can feel commercial and crass to an artist, because it is. But that is also the way the music business runs. The Country Music Association is not going to put out a statement asking country radio to place your hip-hop influenced accordion instrumental on its charts. It doesn't fit the paradigm their market share is predicated on.

As an illustration, one of the beauties and drawbacks of Nashville has been the protection of the "Nashville sound" and what is and what is not "Nashville" sounding.

I have heard that an influential group of recording industry heavyweights including Chet Atkins, Owen Bradley, Billy Rose, and perhaps a few others either formally or informally decided at one point what the

"Nashville sound" was going to be. I don't know how much of that is true but there was a choice made, either collectively or individually, to adhere to certain guidelines.

To Nashville - ize

That code gave the town and the country music market a distinctive "brand," if you will. It was and is enormously successful; similar to the way Harley Davidson motorcycles are recognized far and wide. The Nashville heavyweights are not going to change their brand for you. If you want to work and prosper in Nashville you will have to learn their way.

I have seen and heard many pop writers for instance say they are going to "dumb down" their songs in order to sell to Nashville. Nashville can smell that attitude from a long way off because there is an accent, a language, and a code that is difficult for a foreigner to master.

Faking a Nashville sound works about as well as a British actor's American accent on a BBC television show. It just doesn't ring true. The language of the lyric, the flow of the melody, the inflection of the music, all need to have the characteristics of the genre to seem believable.

One of the reasons that writers who grow up in a genre can write so effectively for that genre is because the codes and language are learned early and become natural. No one had to teach Hank Williams, Sr. what a typical Southerner of the early '50s thought, talked like, or enjoyed. He was one of them. No one had to teach Aretha Franklin the phrasing, attitude, and emotional delivery of the black church in singing gospel. She grew up in it.

I use Nashville as an example here because I know it. Other markets have similar distinctive characteristics whether they are literally spelled out or just understood by consensus by the arbiters of taste for that genre.

It is important for a writer who wants to be successful in a market to do the research necessary to understand the code, the language, and the parameters of a genre. And know yourself, your strengths and tendencies, your character and approach. If you are trying to work in a genre outside your cultural influence, you will have to do your homework.

Contemporary

Another even more difficult consideration when you're trying to evaluate your song's commercial potential yourself--when pitching from outside a genre--is figuring out, how contemporary is it?

The pop song market is a contemporary market place. As I mentioned before, fashions go in and out, but even a style that lasts a bit longer can wear out its welcome. Unfortunately, the purveyors of a style are usually the last to recognize the anachronistic tendencies of their presentation. It just becomes the way they do it, and to a new generation, that obviously becomes the old way.

I remember once seeing a movie in which a fast talking, cigar chomping, piano playing Brill Building type of songwriter was pitching song after song to a disinterested publisher. The songwriter played one song after another, staccato chorus after chorus, and even though the words would change slightly, every single song sounded the same. To the writer they were all different songs; to the publisher they were the same song over and over.

That is how a style can get. To the one immersed in it there is infinite variety and subtlety, but to an outsider (or professional) it all sounds the same.

Stylize

I like another interesting variation of the word *style* - to *stylize* – to intentionally use the conventions of a genre to calculate the esthetic effect of your song. In other words, write for your market.
Selling out for commercial gain sounds inartistic.
But somehow, to *stylize*, sounds kinda creative.

Considerations:

Is your song stylistically focused?
Where would it fit stylistically?
What artist can your hear doing it?
Can it be classified according to a Billboard chart?
Is there a market for the style your song fits?
Is it current/contemporary for that market?

Notes:

Tickle My Monkey Nerve

Mon - key nerve *(mun'ke nurv)* **n**. *[< Southern American slang] Mischievous, mystical cord like fiber of the central nervous system located at the base of the skull that reacts spontaneously to cool song stimuli and stuff.*

I was asked to participate in a panel once and discuss what I listened for in critically reviewing a song. I don't remember if that was the intent of the panel, but that's what it evolved into. During one of the live critiques of submitted songs I used a phrase that drew more response and questions (as well as commentary) than anything else I said that day.

It was something to the effect that I want a song to "tickle my monkey nerve."

There are as many opinions as there are experts in any given field, and song evaluation is no different. It is a very inexact science. We all bring our experiences, likes and dislikes, and personal criteria to the job of evaluating material. I was struck that day on the panel by the wide range of things other panelists look for in a song (things I never think about), as well as the surprising number of similarities in method.

Some general areas of agreement among the panel that day were: a great demo won't help a mediocre song, good structure won't mask a weak idea, and a simple heartfelt emotion wins over clever craftsmanship every time.

As we were discussing how to polish certain aspects of a song, it struck me that many times we, as writers, work backwards. We think in terms of form instead of content. Is the title catchy? Is the opening line of the first verse strong enough to draw the listener in? Does the pre-chorus build into the chorus? I can never remember if structured thinking is left or right brain, but I'm whichever one it is that wouldn't know. I'm a feel guy.

When I said on the panel that I judged a song by whether or not it tickled my "monkey nerve," I was referring to that spontaneous reaction that sends a shiver down your spine that feels so good. It's just "there." Everything technical in the song might be not quite perfect, but that spark, that phrase, that idea, that melody will just make the listener jump. That little electric "tickling the monkey nerve."

Great singers, great producers, multinational record companies and the entire music business depend on that little quiver. Supply that, and you are in demand.

I learned the phrase in Memphis from Terry Manning. He was a staff producer at Stax Records when he was seventeen, then went on to engineer for Led Zeppelin, and produced ZZ Top, Albert King, and Furry Lewis among many others. He is also a southern American music connoisseur.

Terry said the term came from New Orleans--maybe, maybe not. Wherever it came from, it's when a sound is so good, a feel is so right, a lyric says so much, that you jerk before you think about it. Blues so bad it feels good. It's something in the song that, if you have to explain it, they won't understand it anyway.

I have heard publishers and record company A&R guys comment that the hardest song to critique is a song that is just "good." A lousy song is easy, there are obvious technical flaws to be pointed out and learned from. A great song is also a no-brainer. Any average person on the street can pick a hit song (they are the ones who buy them, remember?)

But a just "good" song, that's a tricky one. Maybe the lyrics are OK, the melody is catchy, and the structure is fine, but nothing grabs you. What can you say? It's there or it's not. It's the "monkey nerve" factor; you're not being tickled.

There are songs that you can critique all day and find things technically wrong with that just grab people anyway. How would a publisher rate the lyric of "Louie, Louie" for example? How about "Achy, Breaky Heart"? It wasn't current sounding when it was new. Doesn't matter, they tickle, you jump.

The monkey nerve tickle is a high, it's a thrill, and like any other high, it's temporary. That's where the craftsmanship of building a good song around the spark comes in. But you can't have a good song without it.

Well-written songs without a good idea are like a relationship with no passion. Everything may look right, but the purpose is missing. And like a relationship, a great song takes work to build. Without the spark somebody loses interest along the way.

Start with tickling your monkey nerve. Does your idea get you excited? Then play your idea for others and watch as they listen. Don't listen to what they say. Not many people will tell you what they really think about your song. You can tell what they think if you watch them as they listen.

Ever notice how different a song sounds the first time you play it for someone else? You can feel what the other person feels. Did the "monkey nerve" get tickled? You don't even have to say, "What do you think?" You already know.

Save yourself some money and time by asking yourself before you demo or pitch a song, "Does this song get me excited? Am I passionate about it? Does it tickle my "monkey nerve"? If you want your song cut, if you want an industry professional to sit up and take notice, if you want the work you do to affect somebody else and communicate to another soul, start by tickling the most important "monkey nerve" in the world--yours.

Notes:

The Zen of Tutti Frutti

As a kid, I vividly remember watching comedian Steve Allen condescendingly reading aloud the lyrics to Little Richard's "Tutti-Frutti" on network television. I have never forgotten the moment, even after all these years. I never heard a song lyric the same way since. I think of that experience often in reading lyrics.

It may have been the first time I ever heard a song lyric read out loud. Steve Allen's intent was sarcastic and comedic; he snickered at the obvious silliness of "a womp-bomp-a-loo-ma-a-womp-bam-boom" with an intellectual arrogance I have never forgotten. He and his audience found the lyric humorously inane. I could see his point, but felt even then, that he was missing the point. I had no idea how far off he was.

Steve Allen had championed Jack Kerouac and the beat poets; pretty out there stuff in the '50s. He claimed often to have written thousands of songs himself, so you'd think his sympathies would be on the side of the artist.

Steve Allen held himself up as an arbiter of intellectual pop culture, and yet he didn't have any idea what he was reading out loud on network television to millions of people. He didn't know, his audience didn't know, the network censors didn't know. At that time I didn't either. But Little Richard surely did.

What shocked me about the Steve Allen moment was the realization that the lyric of the song stood apart literally from the music. Song lyrics and music were connected in a way to me at that time that they made no sense separately. Instrumental style musical tracks of popular Beatles songs, for instance, felt like headless horsemen. They sounded obviously wrong to my ears. The lyric was supported and made relevant by the musical approach.

I did note, even in my naive youth, that Mr. Allen had not chosen a Beatles or a Bob Dylan song--both contemporary at the time--to make his point. Perhaps he realized that by reading certain words, he could be culturally distanced enough that John Lennon would be heard mocking Mr. Allen's mocking as he attempted to read, let's say, perhaps, "I Am The Walrus" - irony can be generational. And Mr. Allen thought of himself, I am sure, as nobody's intellectual fool.

But, from that moment, I determined that any lyric I wrote (for I was a songwriter even then--I knew it) would stand up to the "Steve Allen" test. What would my lyric sound like being read on network television? Would the artistic intent and integrity carry it, or would it sound simplistic and trite?

Codes in Lyrics

I referenced at the beginning of this book the important influence of the black experience in this country and its effect on American popular music.

From their earliest days in this country, African-Americans have communicated in code. Throughout history, many oppressed minorities have developed codes that the oppressed understand and the oppressors do not. It's a method of inside communication.

If you look at almost any subculture, you will find it has a way of communicating that only its members understand. This form of communication may be through words, symbols, gestures, clothing styles--or any number of other ways--but there is an exclusivity that empowers the smaller, less powerful group.

In some cases these codes are picked up by the fringes of the larger culture and assimilated, yet the true original meaning of the codes often goes missing. Terms like "rock and roll", and "jazz", had quite a different meaning to the black subculture they came from than what they later came to mean in the white culture that assimilated them.

The Steve Allens, and even the white kids and parents who popularized the terms, rarely knew what these code words meant literally in the black community from which they were lifted.

Even in the contemporary music business each category of music has its code. Whether it's pop, blues, jazz, hip-hop,

Contemporary Christian, country, each genre has its own internal language and forms that maintain its identity, communicate to its members, and in some cases exclude outsiders.

Layers

There are also layers of understanding in lyrics and life in general. We all do not see or hear things in the same way. Steve Allen and his audience heard that Little Richard lyric as inane silliness, while the teenage rock audience heard an attitude. It meant something not apparent outside the subculture.

Little Richard and the original black R&B audience heard something else entirely.

Communication

What is the point? Communication. Does your audience understand what you are trying to say? If you are writing songs only for yourself and your own satisfaction then you can write cryptically if you want. Write in Greek if you'd like, it won't matter except to Greek listeners. But if you are writing for an audience that speaks only French—and if you want to communicate your idea to them--it's probably a good idea to write the lyric in French.

Which gets to the point, the purpose of a lyric in a song. It is that communication, conversationally and in the imagery, of the idea of the song. The lyric is the writer's main means of communicating the purpose of the song to the intended audience.

As I listen to a song I try to understand not only what the writer is actually saying, but what the writer means, or intended to say. Clarity of idea and true craftsmanship in communication lyrically is a very rare thing.

Do You Have Something To Say?

Never before has it been so easy for a writer to assemble a good, professional sounding music track. Computer software programs, home studios, and advances in musical hardware have made recording increasingly sophisticated and accessible to writers. Sample CDs, loops, and downloadable musicians have put the best studio musicians at the average songwriter's beck and call 24 hours a day.

But you can't sample an original idea (well, you can, but by definition once it's copied it isn't original anymore). You can't coherently express, deliver, and emotionally communicate a feeling lyrically without knowing what you are trying to say and without being aware of the feeling on some level.

This reminds me of the scene from the film "Rumblefish" where Matt Dillon's character says to Mickey Rourke's character, Motorcycle Boy: "We would have followed you anywhere."

Motorcycle Boy responds, "But a leader has to have somewhere to go."

If you want your listener to follow you, you need somewhere to go--if you want your listener to listen--you need something to say.

There are structures and forms in songwriting--the codes, if you will--both musical and lyrical that are used over and over again in every genre. But unless the writer brings a unique perspective and has a focused idea and emotional purpose to communicate, the song ends up being just another exercise in sticking together clichés and imagery that have been used and overused, to say something that nobody really needs or wants to hear in that way again.

How Well Are You Saying It?

Imagery is a very important element in expressing emotions through words. Rain has been used forever metaphorically for tears, the color "blue" is a standard metaphor for a feeling, "hitting the road' has been used as a symbolic gesture of leaving. These are all very valid and useful ways of expressing ideas more vividly than a literal, dry reading of fact could do. That's why they call it "poetry".

But too often I hear a mixing of metaphors and ideas in lyrics that writers assume the listener will understand based on a song's context, even though a literal following of the lyric leads mainly to confusion. "I'm going to hit the road, travel on down the tracks" is a recent example. They are different modes of travel. I suppose these metaphors mean the person is leaving, but mixing them unfocuses the listener's attention on the emotion and forces an intellectual reconciliation of imagery. That's not good for vibe or continuity.

Different genres have different languages. I hear country writers trying to write gospel or contemporary Christian for instance using words and language that are not part of the lexicon in those genres. It's like a Southern accent in Brooklyn, it sticks out. It's a matter of communication.

Does Your Audience Get It?

Which brings us back to Steve Allen and communication. Mr. Allen read a lyric on national television that he thought he understood, and he was confident of his artistic and intellectual superiority; arrogantly so. But the irony is that he and his audience had no idea what the song was about. They were not the people to whom Richard Penniman was communicating. Little Richard's core R&B audience knew;

his secondary teenage audience didn't care. Little Richard had to be laughing at the silly people laughing at his little ditty. Steve Allen and his audience had no idea what the song was about.

Do you?

Even better, do you know what your song is about, and does your listener?